BIBLE SECRETS REVEALED

 Publications International, Ltd.

Cover Photo: Henry G. Nepomuceno

Donald Vaughan is a freelance writer whose work has appeared in *CURE* magazine, *Military Officer Magazine,* and *Writer's Digest.* He is also a contributor to *Armchair Reader: Fascinating Bible Facts* and *500 Things to Do Before You Kick the Bucket.*

UNLOCKING THE MYSTERIES IN THE BIBLE

The Bible has been a limitless source of comfort and inspiration for millions of faithful Christians throughout the ages. Within the pages of the Old and New Testaments can be found the commanding words of the early prophets, the spiritual guidance of Jesus Christ, and the faithful and compassionate workings of God Almighty.

No matter how many times we read the Bible, there's always something new to learn—that's because the two Testaments are rich in astounding secrets just waiting to be discovered. Some are telling tidbits about life in ancient times, while others help explain stories of spiritual discovery and fulfillment that are just as important today as when they were first written. There are a lot of intriguing fun facts, too, some of which are common knowledge, others less so.

Bible Secrets Revealed examines a host of mysterious questions, including: Where was the Garden of Eden located? Did Noah really take two of every species onto the ark? How much gold was there in King Solomon's temple? How could Jonah survive three days inside a whale? What was the balm of Gilead? Was Jesus a political rabble-rouser? Did he really carry the wooden cross upon which he was crucified? And why did Peter ask to be crucified upside down?

These and many other probing questions about the Bible can be found in the pages of this book, and the answers may astound you. But with every new fact gleaned comes a greater understanding of God's wondrous plan.

Does the Bible tell us where the Garden of Eden was located?

Not specifically, but Scripture does give us some thought-provoking clues. The writer of Genesis tells us only that God's paradise was located "in the east." The Bible does mention, however, that a river flowed from it and divided into four head streams: the Tigris, the Euphrates, the Gihon, and the Pishon. Two of these rivers—the Tigris and the Euphrates—still flow today in Iraq and Iran.

The locations of the Gihon and the Pishon are more uncertain. The Gihon, according to Genesis 2:13, flowed "around the whole land of Cush" (NRSV), which would put it in modern-day Sudan. The Pishon, meanwhile, flowed "around the whole land of Havilah" (verse 11, NRSV), a gold-rich region believed to be located in the Arabian peninsula.

Some scholars believe a dry riverbed in Iraq known as Wadi Batin might be associated with the Pishon because it runs into the head of the Persian Gulf at the junction of the other three biblical rivers. Interestingly, satellite photos have revealed an underground river running below it. Indeed, many experts believe the headwaters of the Persian Gulf, where the four rivers intersect, is the most likely location of the Garden of Eden. The trick, of course, will be uncovering it.

❧ ❧ ❧

What are cherubim and seraphim?

Cherubim and seraphim are two types of angelic creatures—mysterious beings that are neither human nor divine.

Cherubim, which are frequently depicted in medieval art as chubby little babies, are sometimes mentioned in the Bible as fierce guardians. In Genesis, for example, the Lord God placed cherubim using a large flaming sword on the east side of Eden to guard the path to the Tree of Life after the Lord had expelled Adam and Eve from the garden of Eden. Not much like babies after all!

Seraphim, meanwhile, are winged creatures who, among other things, sing perpetual praise to God. For example, the prophet Isaiah noted, "In the year that King Uzziah died, I saw the Lord sitting on a throne, high and lofty; and the hem of his robe filled the temple. Seraphs were in attendance above him; each had six wings: with two they covered their faces, and with two they covered their feet, and with two they flew. And one called to another and said: 'Holy, holy, holy is the Lord of hosts; the whole earth is full of his glory'" (Isaiah 6:1–3, NRSV).

Scholars have long sought to explain the identities of cherubim and seraphim but with little success. One reason may be that these mystical creatures are simply beyond human comprehension.

⚜   ⚜   ⚜

Did Cain marry his own sister?

The writer of Genesis tells us that "Cain knew his wife, and she conceived and bore Enoch" (4:17, NRSV). Considering how few people were around back then, it seems that Cain had no choice but to marry one of his sisters.

The Bible doesn't explicitly state where Cain met his wife. In fact, it isn't until after the birth of his brother, Seth, that the Bible mentions sisters at all. "The days of Adam after he became the father of Seth were eight hundred years; and he had other sons and daughters" (Genesis 5:4, NRSV). Is the Bible telling us that daughters were only born much later to Adam and Eve? Possibly, but probably not. It's more likely that the birth times and names of Adam and Eve's daughters are not mentioned in the Bible because of the nature of ancient patriarchal society, which often excluded women from genealogical lists.

It's also important to note that the Bible compresses a large segment of time. Adam was 130 years old when Seth was born, which means he could have fathered several daughters before then. In any case, it is quite likely that Cain did marry one of the many daughters of Adam and Eve.

⚜ ⚜ ⚜

Did Noah really bring two of each animal onto the Ark?

The story of Noah's Ark is one of the best known in the Old Testament. Indeed, most of us who attended Sunday school recall that Noah filled his ark with two of every animal . . . or did he?

A closer reading of the Bible shows this common belief to be inaccurate. According to Genesis 7:2–3, God actually instructed Noah to "take with you seven each of every clean animal, a male and his female; two each of animals that *are* unclean, a male and his female; also seven each of birds of the air, male and female, to keep the species alive on the face of all the earth" (NKJV™).

Regardless of whether it was one pair or seven, that's still a lot of animals to fit into a boat 450 feet long, 75 feet wide, and 45 feet high, but Noah managed to do it. The bigger question, of course, was how did he keep his sea-going wards from eating each other? And that we can't answer.

⚜ ⚜ ⚜

Was the Tower of Babel actually a Babylonian ziggurat?

The Towel of Babel, the writer of Genesis tells us, was constructed in the land of Shinar. Its creators hoped to make a name for themselves by building a great tower with its top in the heavens. This idea didn't sit well with God, who scattered abroad those involved and created multiple languages in an attempt to keep humankind confused.

But what exactly was the tower itself? Experts now believe it was a ziggurat, a large, pyramid-like structure that played an important role throughout Mesopotamian civilization. Ancient texts reveal that ziggurats were commonly dedicated to a city's patron god or goddess, but their exact function remains a mystery. Some experts believed that early on the structures were tombs of kings or gods or were towering altars erected to protect local citizens against natural disasters and thieves.

More recently, scholars have theorized that ziggurats were built to serve as the doorway through which the local god or goddess passed to the earthly plane. This is suggested by their names, such as the ziggurat at Larsa, which was known as "The Temple That Links Heaven and Earth." If true, this may also help explain why the Tower of Babel offended God, for it attempted to bring human beings to the level of the Lord.

⚜ ⚜ ⚜

Why did God allow Satan into heaven after he had been cast out?

God has an interesting relationship with Satan in the Bible. Though Satan is the antithesis of righteousness, the two occasionally get together to discuss various topics and even engage in a wager or two.

Perhaps the most famous of these bets involves Job, someone whose faith is severely tested after God boasts to Satan about what a faithful servant Job is. "Does Job fear God for nothing?" Satan replied. "Have you not put a hedge around him and his household and everything he has? You have blessed the work of his hands, so that his flocks and herds are spread throughout the land. But now stretch out your hand and strike everything he has, and he will surely curse you to your face" (Job 1:9–11, NIV).

Confident of Job's faithfulness, God allows Satan to put him to the test. In short order, Job loses everything, including his ten children, who perish when their house collapses during a storm. But Job stands strong, so Satan punishes him further by afflicting him with painful boils and other maladies. All of this makes Job's wife and friends wonder what he did to deserve such treatment.

Pushed to the limit, Job starts to question God, who pays him a little visit and admonishes him for his presumptuousness. Chastened, Job repents, and God, in his mercy, doubles the blessings Job had before. Thus God shows Satan not only that a human can have faith despite suffering severe tragedies and hardships but also that he is omnipotent and compassionate.

⚜ ⚜ ⚜

How and why did Abraham try to save Sodom and Gomorrah?

Sodom and Gomorrah were the original "sin cities." In fact, the people who lived there were so sinful that their actions attracted the wrath of God, who decided his only recourse was to destroy them with fire and brimstone.

According to Genesis, Abraham learned of God's plan when God and two angels visited him. Disturbed by the prospect of Sodom's annihilation since Lot, his nephew, was living there, Abraham begged for its salvation by asking God if he would spare the city if he could find 50 righteous people. God agreed. Then Abraham asked God if he would spare the city if he could find 40, then 30, and finally 10 righteous people. God said, "I will not destroy *it* for the sake of ten" (Genesis 18:32, NKJV™).

Sadly, Sodom was such a terrible place that not even ten righteous people lived there. Two angels visited Sodom and informed Lot of the city's impending doom. They urged Lot and his family to flee the city and not look back. Lot's wife, however, glanced over her shoulder as fire consumed the city. She was immediately turned into a pillar of salt.

⚜ ⚜ ⚜

How much gold was there in King Solomon's temple?

King Solomon was extremely rich, and he made good use of his wealth in furnishing the temple to honor God. In the first book of Kings, we are told that Solomon "covered the inside of the temple with pure gold, and he extended gold chains across the front of the inner sanctuary, which was overlaid with gold. So he overlaid the whole interior with gold. He also overlaid with gold the altar that belonged to the inner sanctuary" (1 Kings 6:21–22, NIV).

But that's not all. According to the Bible, practically everything in the temple was also made of gold, including hundreds of shields, an ivory throne overlaid with gold, and all drinking vessels and tableware. That's a huge amount of gold, which is why some Bible scholars speculate that the biblical description is exaggerated. Many believe that certain objects were merely gold-plated and that gold paint, rather than actual gold, was applied to the temple walls.

⚜ ⚜ ⚜

Why is the color purple significant in the Bible?

Back in biblical times, the color purple signified elegance and wealth. It is noted as the color of the tabernacle furnishings in Israelite temples, and priests were required to have purple in their clothing.

The color purple is mentioned often throughout the Bible. Proverbs tells us that a good wife is worthy of being clothed in purple, and in the New Testament story of the rich man and Lazarus, the rich man is described as "clothed in purple and fine linen" (Luke 16:19, KJV). In addition, Jesus is clad in a purple robe during his trial when the Romans attempted to mock his kingship, and in Acts, Lydia, a respected Christian woman, is described as being a "dealer in purple cloth" (Acts 16:14, NIV).

Purple was associated with wealth in ancient times because it was a very difficult dye to acquire. The colorful compound came from just one source—the murex, a mollusk native to the eastern Mediterranean. Each murex contained a very small amount of dye, which had to be laboriously removed by hand. Thus it took a lot of murex to produce enough dye to color a garment. As a result, only the very rich could afford it.

⚜ ⚜ ⚜

What was the balm of Gilead?

A balm is an aromatic resin that was used in biblical times for medicinal or cosmetic purposes. The balm of Gilead is mentioned in the Book of Jeremiah in which the prophet, longing for the spiritual renewal of his fellow Judeans, asks, "Is there no balm in Gilead? Is there no physician there? Why then has the health of my poor people not been restored?" (Jeremiah 8:22, NRSV).

We know that the balm of Gilead was a medicinal salve also used to anoint the kings of Israel. But what was it made of? According to the Talmud, a detailed interpretation of the Hebrew Bible, the balm of Gilead was balsam. This makes sense because balsam was an oil believed to have almost miraculous properties, including the healing of wounds.

According to Josephus, a first-century Jewish historian, balsam trees were brought to Israel as a gift from the Queen of Sheba to King Solomon. This may be loosely inferred in the first book of Kings, which states that Sheba presented Solomon with "one hundred and twenty talents of gold, spices in great quantity, and precious stones. There never again came such abundance of spices as the queen of Sheba gave to King Solomon" (1 Kings 10:10, NKJV™).

⚜ ⚜ ⚜

Where is the Ark of the Covenant hidden?

That's a question that has puzzled biblical scholars for centuries. Theories abound, but no one knows for sure.

According to the second book of Maccabees, the prophet Jeremiah, at the time of the fall of Jerusalem in 586 B.C., went to the mountain that Moses had ascended, loaded the Ark, its tent, and altar of incense into a cave and sealed it up. When his followers tried to mark the location, he stopped them, saying, "The place shall remain unknown until God gathers his people together again" (2 Maccabees 2:7, NRSV).

Many have theorized that the ark was hidden somewhere on or around Mount Nebo, where Moses died. Investigators, however, have found nothing to prove this theory. Others believe the Ark was hidden at Qumran, the settlement near where the Dead Sea scrolls were uncovered. But again, extensive excavation of the region has turned up nothing.

It's also possible that the Ark was hidden beneath the Temple Mount, where it waits for the temple to be rebuilt. It is thought that King Solomon, who built the first temple, foresaw a time when the Ark would need to be hidden. Thus he carved an underground chamber for that purpose.

⚜ ⚜ ⚜

Did God halt the sun and the moon during the conquest of Canaan?

Yes, according to the Book of Joshua. The problem is that the story is impossible to verify.

Joshua was Moses' right-hand man during the Exodus, and he became the leader of the Israelites following Moses' death. He led the Israelites in the conquest of Canaan, which included a lengthy battle against the combined forces of the five kings of the Amorites. During this battle, God helped Joshua by smiting enemy soldiers with large hailstones and causing the sun and the moon to stand still so the battle could be concluded in daylight.

The writer of Joshua 10:12–14 tells it all. Joshua spoke to the Lord and said, "Sun, stand thou still upon Gibeon; and thou, Moon, in the valley of Ajalon" (verse 12, KJV). It was a fantastic request, but Joshua had fantastic faith in the Lord.

God held the sun "until the people had avenged themselves upon their enemies.... The sun stood still in the midst of heaven, and hasted not to go down about a whole day. And there was no day like that before it or after it, that the Lord hearkened unto the voice of a man; for the Lord fought for Israel" (verses 13–14, KJV). So concludes what may be the first recorded incidence of daylight savings time.

❧ ❧ ❧

Is it possible for a person to be swallowed by a whale and live to tell the tale?

Let's get one thing straight right off the bat: A whale did not swallow Jonah. The Bible tells us that "a large fish" (Jonah 1:17, NRSV) swallowed him, which is something entirely different. More importantly, "the Lord *provided* a large fish" (emphasis added) for that purpose, which explains why Jonah was able to spend several days in its belly and survive. In other words, Jonah survived because of divine intervention.

Jonah ended up in the fish's belly because he disobeyed God by refusing to go to Nineveh, a particularly wicked Assyrian city, to preach repentance. Instead, Jonah booked passage on a ship going in the opposite direction. It wasn't that Jonah was afraid to go to the capital of this mighty empire; Jonah didn't want God to be merciful to this pagan people if they repented. And so, a tremendous storm broke out, threatening everyone on board. Jonah then instructed the crew to toss him overboard to make it stop. They reluctantly did so, and it was then that the fish swallowed Jonah.

Jonah spent three days and nights inside the fish, praying for guidance. After the fish finally vomited him on dry land, God again ordered him to travel to Nineveh. This time Jonah did as he was told. As a result, the people of Nineveh repented of their wicked ways and were spared God's wrath.

⚜ ⚜ ⚜

Why are there so many people named Herod in the New Testament?

There do appear to be a lot of rulers named Herod in the pages of the New Testament, but there's a good explanation for that: Herod wasn't a name, it was a title assumed by Herod the Great's descendants. It's similar to the many Roman emperors who came after Julius Caesar and took the title of "Caesar."

That said, there would have been many more people actually named Herod had Herod the Great not murdered a number of his family. Among them were his Hasmonean wife Miriam, their two sons Alexander and Aristobulus, and a son by another of his wives named Antipater.

When Herod the Great died, his surviving sons, Archelaus, Antipas, and Philip, fought over his kingdom. Augustus Caesar finally intervened, dividing the land equally among them. Archelaus was given Judea, Samaria, and Idumea, and it was fear of Archelaus, who was just as wicked as his father, that caused Joseph, Mary, and Jesus to flee to Nazareth in Galilee.

Antipas wasn't much better. Referred to as "that fox" (Luke 13:32, NRSV) by Jesus, he was responsible for the death of John the Baptist. The rule of Philip, on the other hand, was apparently peaceful and relatively uneventful.

⚜ ⚜ ⚜

When was Jesus born?

The Gregorian calendar, which Pope Gregory XIII instituted in 1582, is the most commonly used civil calendar in the world. It rectified a few problems inherent in earlier calendars and continued the previous year-numbering system, which began with the presumed birth date of Jesus.

But don't take the Gregorian calendar as accurate regarding the year Jesus was born; most Bible scholars acknowledge that the accepted date of Jesus' birth is probably off by a few years.

The Bible provides some interesting historical details about the life of Jesus that help establish the date of his birth, but only in broad terms. We know, for example, that his birth occurred "in the days of Herod, the king of Judea" (Luke 1:5, NKJV™), who ruled from 37 B.C. to 4 B.C., so Jesus could not have been born after 4 B.C. when King Herod died.

In addition, the Book of Matthew tells us that Herod met with the wise men from the East who came to Jerusalem looking for the newborn king of the Jews (see Matthew 2:1–12). These wise men had followed a star and wanted to pay homage to this special child. They then went to Bethlehem to bring gifts to Jesus, but they did not return to Jerusalem, having been warned in a dream of Herod's treachery.

If we assume that the wise men arrived in Jerusalem a year or so before Herod died, then we can reason that Jesus' birth was probably sometime between 7 and 5 B.C.

⚜ ⚜ ⚜

How many wise men visited Jesus after his birth?

The commonly accepted number is three, but in truth, we really don't know.

Matthew provides some details about these "wise men": "Wise men from the East came to Jerusalem, saying, 'Where is He who has been born King of the Jews? For we have seen His star in the East and have come to worship Him'" (Matthew 2:1–2, NKJV™).

What Matthew doesn't tell us is their exact number, though tradition assumes there were three because three gifts were presented to Jesus. These gifts included gold, frankincense, and myrrh (see verse 11).

So who were these mysterious men from the East? Most likely they were professional astrologers. Almost certainly they were not royalty, though they did get an audience with Herod. It's also unlikely that their names were Balthasar, Melchior, and Caspar—names that were added to the story much later.

It's commonly believed that the wise men arrived very shortly after Jesus' birth, but some historians believe they showed up much later. One hint of this is the fact that Herod orders the death of all children under the age of two, and not just newborns (see verse 16).

⚜ ⚜ ⚜

Was Jesus really born in a barn?

The traditional nativity scene, in which the baby Jesus is pictured lying in what appears to be a hay-lined trough, surrounded by his parents, shepherds, and farm animals, is one of the most iconic images in Christianity. It's also somewhat inaccurate, say scholars. In fact, Jesus probably wasn't born in a barn as we think of them today.

One must remember that very few cities in ancient times had commercial hotels where travelers could stay for the night. People rarely ventured far from home, and when they did, they usually stayed with relatives or friends. That's probably what happened with Joseph and Mary—except that they didn't get the best guest room, which may already have been occupied by someone of more impressive social standing.

Instead, Joseph and Mary were probably offered shelter in some kind of protected interior stable. This might have been a separate first-floor area where the animals were kept or perhaps even a natural cave, which was commonly used to shelter animals back then. All of these scenarios would explain why Jesus was placed in a manger upon his birth; it was the most convenient cradle available. In any case, the location of Jesus' birth was certainly humble for the Son of God.

⚜   ⚜   ⚜

Was Jesus the only Messiah?

During the time in which Jesus lived as a man, there was high expectation among the Jewish people as to who would deliver them from Roman domination and bring about a much-needed spiritual renewal. In fact, the New Testament mentions other men who some thought could be the promised Messiah.

Some people thought that John the Baptist, whose baptism of Jesus preceded Christ's public ministry, might be that Messiah. He preached and baptized people in the region near the Jordan River, and he drew impressive crowds. According to Luke, "the people were waiting expectantly and were all wondering in their hearts if John might possibly be the Messiah" (Luke 3:15, NIV).

Of course, John knew better, adamantly denying that he was the Messiah and telling those who followed him, "I indeed baptize you with water; but One mightier than I is coming, whose sandal strap I am not worthy to loose. He will baptize you with the Holy Spirit and fire" (verse 16, NKJV™).

Other potential Messiah candidates include a man named Theudas, who appeared after the time of Jesus and an unnamed Egyptian who managed to gather thousands of disciples. But none held a candle to the true Messiah—that is, Jesus Christ.

⚜ ⚜ ⚜

Was Jesus a rabble-rouser?

Not intentionally, though Jesus' message often sparked outrage against him. On one occasion when he visited his hometown, he read the following passage from the prophecy of Isaiah to the citizens of Nazareth: "The Spirit of the Lord is upon me, because he has anointed me to bring good news to the poor. He has sent me to proclaim release to the captives and recovery of sight to the blind, to let the oppressed go free, to proclaim the year of the Lord's favor" (Luke 4:18–19, NRSV; see Isaiah 61:1–2). Jesus then went on to rebuke his listeners for their hardness of heart. They became enraged with him and tried to throw him off a cliff. This incident certainly caused quite a stir, and no doubt it was talked about throughout the region.

Meanwhile, Jesus steadfastly refused to let himself be cast as a political messiah—that is, one who would lead Israel out from under Roman oppression. That simply wasn't his calling, which is why he upbraided those who came to arrest him in the Garden of Gethsemane by asking, "Am I leading a rebellion, that you have come with swords and clubs?" (Luke 22:52, NIV). Later, when Pontius Pilate asked him if he regarded himself as the king of the Jews, Jesus answered, "My kingdom is not of this world. If My kingdom were of this world, My servants would fight, so that I should not be delivered to the Jews; but now My kingdom is not from here" (John 18:36, NKJV™).

Jesus' mission on earth was spiritual, not political. Rather than lead a revolt against those who held power, he sought to lead the people of the world toward redemption and eternal salvation.

⚜ ⚜ ⚜

Did Jesus really carry the cross upon which he was crucified?

The popular image of Jesus being forced by the Romans to carry the wooden cross upon which he is to be crucified exemplifies a core tenet of the Christian faith—that Jesus died for our sins in an especially horrific way. But is that image historically accurate?

Most scholars believe the answer is only partly correct. It's likely that Jesus carried only the crossbeam because the center post was probably the trunk of a tree, which would have been too heavy for one man to transport on his back. It's also likely that the cross upon which Jesus was crucified was reused because wood was extremely scarce in Jerusalem at the time. In fact, the Jewish historian Josephus notes that during the siege of Jerusalem in A.D. 70, the Romans had to travel as far as ten miles to gather enough wood for their siege machinery.

Death by crucifixion was especially cruel; most of the condemned slowly died from physical trauma, asphyxiation, dehydration, loss of blood, and exposure to the elements. That's why Josephus referred to crucifixion as "the most wretched of deaths."

⚜ ⚜ ⚜

When was Jesus really crucified?

Because historians are unsure when Jesus was exactly born, they're also unsure when he exactly died. But they have a fairly good idea.

Luke tells us that Jesus was about 30 years old when he began his ministry (see Luke 3:23). We also know that three, possibly four Passovers, which are celebrated once a year, took place during the time of Jesus' public work. If that's true, Jesus would have been around 33 when he was crucified on the cross.

As for the exact year, most biblical scholars put it at either A.D. 28 or 29 when Pontius Pilate was prefect of Judea. The Gospel of Luke confirms this by noting that John the Baptist, whose baptism of Jesus marked the beginning of Jesus' ministry, started his own ministry "in the fifteenth year of the reign of Emperor Tiberius, when Pontius Pilate was governor of Judea, and Herod was ruler of Galilee" (Luke 3:1, NRSV. The Herod mentioned in this verse was not Herod the Great, but his son Antipas, who inherited the title "Herod.")

A little historical digging reveals that the 15th year of Tiberius's rule was A.D. 28–29. Most historians accept that as the year of Jesus' crucifixion, but they acknowledge that we'll probably never know with certainty.

⚜   ⚜   ⚜

Is the Shroud of Turin actually the cloth that wrapped Jesus' dead body?

That depends on whom you talk to. Many devout Catholics believe the famous linen cloth to be the shroud Jesus was wrapped in when he was entombed following his crucifixion. Others, however, are skeptical.

The shroud first appeared in 1357, when it was displayed in the French village of Lirey. In 1452 or 1453, the shroud became the property of the House of Savoy, which held legal title until 1983. Today, it resides in a locked chest in the Royal Chapel of the Cathedral of St. John in Turin, Italy.

Interestingly, the shroud, which many claim contains the image of Jesus, has never been proclaimed by the Catholic Church to be the actual burial cloth of Jesus. In fact, the church has exhibited great caution regarding the artifact's origin.

Numerous tests have been conducted on the shroud in an effort to confirm its origin and authenticity. Some researchers have concluded that the image on the cloth possesses unique properties, but exactly how and when the shroud was made remains a mystery. To date, scientists continue to disagree as to whether the shroud is real or some kind of medieval hoax.

⚜ ⚜ ⚜

Where is the tomb of Jesus located?

Scholars have narrowed the site of Jesus' crucifixion, burial, and resurrection to two possibilities. The first is the Garden Tomb, which Charles Gordon, a British general, discovered in 1883. During a trip to Jerusalem, Gordon noticed that the caves on the side of a particular hill resembled the eye sockets of a skull. He then deduced that the hill was Golgotha, which means "skull."

Excavation of the area uncovered a tomb, above which appeared to be the sign of the cross. Archaeologists also found a large cistern that some believe was used to water a garden located on the site. This is significant because the Book of John notes that Mary Magdalene initially mistook the resurrected Jesus for a gardener.

Another possible site is the Church of the Holy Sepulchre. Although this church is located inside the present-day walls of Jerusalem, it was outside the city walls as they stood during ancient times.

Archaeologists have confirmed that the site used to be a quarry, which was later filled in and turned into a garden. In addition, the discovery of several tombs dating from the first century A.D. confirms that the area was used as a cemetery during the time of Jesus.

⚜ ⚜ ⚜

Were all of Jesus' apostles martyred?

Hand-selected by Jesus himself, most of the apostles took very seriously their mission to spread the gospel throughout the world following Jesus' death. And because of their unwavering faith in Christ, most were martyred.

One exception is the Apostle John. Although he was tortured for his faith and exiled to a primitive island, he died of natural causes about the age of 100. The brother of James the Greater, John was a fisherman and disciple of John the Baptist when Jesus invited him to join his ministry. He was there for most of the transforming events in Jesus' life, including the transfiguration and Jesus' torment in the Garden of Gethsemane. He was also specifically instructed by Jesus, while Jesus was dying on the cross, to care for Mary, Jesus' mother, who was standing next to him.

The other apostles all met with horrific fates as they traveled spreading the gospel. James the Greater was the first to die for his beliefs, martyred by the sword in A.D. 44. Bartholomew was scourged and beheaded for his evangelism; Simon the Zealot was sawed in half, and James the Lesser was either stoned to death or tossed from the top of a temple in Jerusalem.

One other original apostle was Judas. He died gruesomely, but not as a martyr.

⚜ ⚜ ⚜

How did Judas Iscariot die?

That's a difficult question to answer because the Bible offers two accounts of how Judas, the man who betrayed Jesus to the high priests for 30 pieces of silver and is known as the ultimate betrayer, died.

Matthew says that after Judas realized that Jesus was condemned to die, he repented, tried to return the blood money, and subsequently hanged himself out of guilt (see Matthew 27:1–5).

Luke, however, gives a seemingly different account, reporting that Judas bought a field with the reward money then fell headlong to the ground, where "he burst open in the middle and all his entrails gushed out. And it became known to all those dwelling in Jerusalem; so that field is called in their own language, Akel Dama, that is, Field of Blood" (Acts 1:18–19, NKJV™).

So which was it: hanging or gut-busting? Some scholars speculate that it may have been a combination of both.

There are numerous ancient olive trees along the steep hillsides and cliffs of the Hinnom Valley, which was the site of Akel Dama, so it's conceivable that Judas tied a rope to one of them and jumped to his death. But if the rope did not hold, his body could have fallen down the cliff and been disemboweled, perhaps by a sharp rock. The result: two causes of death in one.

❧ ❧ ❧

Did God speak through the drawing of lots during biblical times?

Today, the drawing of lots seems like an unusual way to make a decision or divine certain facts, but back in biblical times, it was commonly used. In fact, the Bible itself speaks of the drawing of lots in determining God's will.

The division of the Promised Land among the 12 tribes of Israel, for example, was determined by choosing lots for each tribe. And when the Israelites were thwarted in their attack against the city of Ai, Joshua drew lots to establish the guilt of Achan, who had hidden stolen booty in his tent, the cause of their defeat. Also, in the New Testament, among other examples, Jesus' apostles drew lots to select a replacement for Judas, who had betrayed Jesus and committed suicide.

This was much more than simple chance in the eyes of the ancients. Back then, it was commonly believed that God revealed his will through the drawing of lots, or the use of Urim and Thummim, a similar technique employed by Jewish priests to ask questions of the Lord.

Indeed, the drawing of lots was preferable to making a decision through logic or reasoning because it eliminated the possibility of human error in determining the will of God. Proverbs 16:33 affirms, "The lot is cast into the lap, but its every decision is from the Lord" (NIV).

⚜ ⚜ ⚜

Why couldn't Paul, who healed many others, cure his own physical malady?

The Apostle Paul was a remarkable man. Not only was he capable of healing others, but he also experienced numerous miraculous healings of his own. For example, Acts describes an incident in which Paul was stoned, dragged outside the city walls, and left for dead. But after his disciples gathered around him, he got up, dusted himself off, and went back into the city. On another occasion, a poisonous snake bit him, but he suffered no ill effects.

There was, however, one ailment from which Paul couldn't recover; it was a problem he called his "thorn in the flesh." Some scholars believe it may have been a type of vision problem because he once wrote, "See what large letters I use as I write to you with my own hand!" (Galatians 6:11, NIV). Nevertheless, what that "thorn" was remains a mystery.

What we do know is that Paul considered his ailment God's way of keeping him humble. "To keep me from becoming conceited," he said, "I was given a thorn in my flesh, a messenger of Satan, to torment me. Three times I pleaded with the Lord to take it away from me. But he said to me, 'My grace is sufficient for you, for my power is made perfect in weakness.' Therefore I will boast all the more gladly about my weaknesses, so that Christ's power may rest on me" (2 Corinthians 12:7–9, NIV).

⚜ ⚜ ⚜

Why did Peter ask to be crucified upside down?

As discussed earlier, most of Jesus' apostles were martyred as a result of their evangelism. With regard to Peter and Paul, the Roman Emperor Nero put them to death soon after a famous fire consumed Rome in A.D. 64. After torching the Roman capital, Nero placed the blame on the followers of Jesus, and a severe persecution of Christians subsequently ensued.

When Peter was sentenced to death, he knew a greater reward awaited him in heaven; but when he was told that he would be crucified, as Jesus had been, he balked. He didn't ask his captors to spare him. Instead, he asked that he be crucified upside down.

This probably seemed like a strange request to his executioners, but Peter had an excellent reason; he felt himself unworthy of experiencing the exact kind of death that had been inflicted upon his master. Historical texts indicate that Peter's executioners granted his wish and crucified him upside down.

⚜ ⚜ ⚜

Does the number 666 really identify the Antichrist?

The Book of Revelation tells us that as the end times approach, a mysterious figure of absolute evil will emerge to take over the world and lead a war against God and the forces of heaven. The identifying mark of this Antichrist is the number 666.

So who could that be? Over the years, numerous historical figures have been pegged as the Antichrist, including Napoleon and Adolf Hitler. But some historians believe there's a more logical candidate: Emperor Nero, who persecuted Christians in horrendous ways in the first century A.D.

Back in ancient times, in both Greek and Hebrew, it wasn't unusual to designate someone's name by a number, and that likely was the intention of the Apostle John as he wrote the Book of Revelation. (As another example, early Christian documents sometimes used 888 for the name of Jesus in Greek.)

Giving credence to this theory, the Hebrew translation of the Greek for Caesar Nero adds up to the number 666, though we shouldn't assume that John was saying that Nero was THE Antichrist. It's more probable that he was telling the readers of the early Gospels that Nero, through his horrendous actions against God's people, was a forerunner of the Antichrist to come much later.

⚜ ⚜ ⚜

Does the Book of Revelation have a happy ending?

According to John's vision, a lot of bad stuff happens before we get to the end of the world. Here's an abbreviated version:

Judgment Day, Revelation tells us, culminates in a cosmic fight between good and evil. Good triumphs, but along the way war, famine, and pestilence, not to mention earthquakes and other catastrophes, devastate the world. Moreover, the sun darkens, the moon turns red, and the stars fall from the sky.

Seven angels blow their trumpets in sequence. The first five blasts bring destruction on the earth, the sixth releases four angels who kill a third of humankind, and the seventh joins heaven with what remains of the earth.

War breaks out in heaven, and angels led by the archangel Michael defeat Satan, who is in the form of a seven-headed dragon. Another beast emerges, identified by the number 666. Angels dump bowls of plague, representing God's wrath, over the world and the beast, causing the cities of the world to vanish.

Satan is eventually defeated at Armageddon, which is the beginning of our happy ending, during which God creates a new heaven and a new earth, free from death, pain, and suffering, where the righteous will live forever in God's eternal glory.